The Whimsical Muse

Poetic Play for Busy Creatives

Danell Jones

Two Sylvias Press

Two Sylvias Press
PO Box 1524
Kingston, WA 98346
twosylviaspress@gmail.com

Cover Design: Kelli Russell Agodon
Book Design: Annette Spaulding-Convy
Author Photo: Casey Page

Created with the belief that great writing is good for the world, Two Sylvias Press mixes modern technology, classic style, and literary intellect with an eco-friendly heart. We draw our inspiration from the poetic literary talent of Sylvia Plath and the editorial business sense of Sylvia Beach. We are an independent press dedicated to publishing the exceptional voices of writers.

For more information about Two Sylvias Press please visit:
www.twosylviaspress.com

First Edition. Created in the United States of America.

ISBN: 978-1-948767-12-5

Two Sylvias Press
www.twosylviaspress.com

Introduction

In a perfect world, we would only need one reason to write: because we love it. We would bolt out of bed before dawn, ready to face cold mornings with gusto and blank pages with fearlessness. Ideas would gush forth from us like water from a geyser. We would never be distracted or tired. The laundry would never need to be done, dinner made, the dog walked.

Many of us find our creativity continually waylaid—if it's not overtime, it's childcare; if it's not homework, it's soccer practice. Often the desire to write simply isn't strong enough to defy a world of distractions, especially if we're not sure what we want to say or how to begin. It's easier to focus on one of the other million things we have to do and put our creativity on hold.

The truth is, we need reasons to write. Specific, tangible reasons give creativity a chance against a blustering, attention-grabbing world.

The book you are holding provides eighty-four concrete reasons to write. Eighty-four exercises that you can begin right now. They require no planning or preparation. Just open the book and go. In under a minute, your creative juices will be flowing.

All of the prompts here can be adapted to suit the moment. Each one has two parts: "Quick" and "Lingering." If you are really strapped for time, opt for a "Quick" activity that can be done in a matter of minutes. Don't be surprised if your energy and your spirits lift as you start working. It turns out that getting words on the page ignites our gusto and fearlessness. And I predict it won't take long for you to see your imagination for the remarkable resource it is. Remember: the more you use your imagination, the more imagination you'll have, and the more you'll write.

The "Lingering" part of each prompt provides ideas for extending your poem by developing it or taking it in a new direction. You can do the "Quick" and "Lingering" parts of the prompt together or separately—whichever works best for you.

A key piece of advice about using these prompts: always opt for fun. Give yourself permission to write as freely as possible. Treat the blank page as your playground. Don't worry about grammar, syntax, or even logic. Let yourself be sassy, melodramatic, silly, over-the-top, morose, bitter, or rude. Let your thoughts be fragmented, nonsensical, even ridiculous. "Writing a poem is discovering," Robert Frost tells us. Tap freely into your creativity, and you'll be surprised by what you discover.

Before you begin, let me leave you with three rules for the road:

> Write what you can, when you can.
> Create with pleasure.
> Be gentle with yourself.

Ready to begin? Just open to any page and jump in.

Danell Jones

I have never started a poem yet whose end I knew. Writing a poem is discovering.

~Robert Frost

The best poetry has its roots in the subconscious to a great degree. Youth, naivety, reliance on instinct more than learning and method, a sense of freedom and play, even trust in randomness, is necessary to the making of a poem.

~May Swenson

I don't have a pencil.
I don't have any paper.
My desk is wobbly.
                    ~Bruce Lansky

Quick:

List the reasons why you can't write today. Your reasons can be big or small or both. Feel free to whine or be crabby.

Lingering:

Now create the most outrageous excuses you can imagine for not writing. For example, *creatures from outer space wearing Spiderman jammies are asking for French toast; the laundry you left in the washer has turned into a deadly fungus that threatens the planet; the FBI is at your door asking questions.* Return to the truth if you like, or let yourself be carried away by fantastical justifications.

A poem is a box, a thing, to put other things in. For safe keeping.
    ~Marianne Boruch

Quick:

Imagine your poem as a box. Put something or someone you want to keep safe inside it. Describe his/her/its/their color, smell, texture, sound, or other characteristics. For example, *your pale blue Pinto from college, the one with the dent in the fender; your sister who smells like radishes and cinnamon.*

Lingering:

Imagine your box is larger—you can fit giant things in there: memories, desires, favorite stories. As you put things in this box, look at each of them very carefully, notice telling details, remember stories, scenes. Let your descriptions expand or contract as the spirit takes you.

To get started, I will accept anything that occurs to me.
~William Stafford

Quick:

Poet William Stafford observes that one can conquer a fear of the blank page simply by lowering one's standards. For this exercise, just write—don't think. Jot down the first words that come to mind no matter how silly they are. Use free association to keep writing: let one word suggest another. The goal here is to keep your pen moving across the page, your fingers moving across the keyboard. Try to follow your thoughts as they flit through your mind.

Lingering:

Keep writing, allowing your ideas to develop in unexpected directions. Surrender the need to make logical sense; trust your imagination wherever takes you. Don't judge the results of this exercise right away. Return to it in a few days to discover what treasures your intuitive thinking has left for you. If you find a line or phrase that appeals to you, use it to begin a new poem or to extend a poem-in-progress.

Busy old fool, unruly sun,
Why dost thou thus,
Through windows, and through curtains call on us?
~John Donne

Quick:

The sun is with us every day. What kind of appearance is it making today? Is it bright or covered by clouds? Take a minute to talk to it. You can celebrate, question, or even scold it, as John Donne does.

Lingering:

Spend more time chatting with the sun. You may be doing all the talking—remembering the sunburn you got in eighth grade or wondering where the sunshine was on your wedding day. Or the sun may be talking to you— complimenting your garden, mentioning something about the cleanliness of your windows, or giving you advice about writing poetry (as it does in Frank O'Hara's "Talking to the Sun on Fire Island"). What is the sun saying to you today? What are you saying back?

I love your lips when they're wet with wine
And red with a wild desire;
                    ~Ella Wheeler Wilcox

Quick:

Today is a great day to say what you love. It's easy. Just begin each line of your poem with "I love." As you write, try to be as specific and concrete as possible: *the tippy-tip of your dog's tail as it flourishes its silent—but very lively—song all up and down Third Avenue.*

Lingering:

Continue your list. As you progress, vary the first words of each line by saying, I especially love, I used to love, I want to love, I can't bear to love, and so on.

Poetry is deep gossip.

~Liam Rector

Quick:

Write a little story-poem that sounds like gossip by finishing this sentence in two or three lines: "He could have avoided all the trouble, if only he had…" Take a leap and imagine what "he" (or "she" or "they") should never have done. Asked directions? Bought that lottery ticket? Married "that" person? Have fun! See what unfolds.

Lingering:

Allow the current of a story to carry you away here. Add the voice of another person describing the same events differently. Maybe add lots of voices, each one altering the story to make it more outrageous. Let the spirit of gossip take you to unexpected places.

Adam the goodliest man of men since borne
His Sons, the fairest of her daughters Eve.
Under a tuft of shade that on a green
Stood whispering soft, by a fresh fountain side
                                                    ~John Milton

Quick:

Retell the story of Adam and Eve. Try putting them in a modern setting. Let God tempt them with something they would find irresistible: celebrity, fortune, or a brand-new sports car.

Lingering:

Let's hear from all the major characters. Is Eve sarcastic or sassy? Does the snake talk like a used-car salesman? And Adam? Straight-laced? Goofy? Shy?

What do the dancing white birds say
Looking down upon burnt meadows?
All that you think is rain is not.

~Hafiz, the Great Sufi Master

Quick:

Go outside and listen to the sounds of nature around you: birds singing, dogs barking, the wind through trees, rain, and so on. Now imaginatively translate these sounds into English. Don't worry if they don't make sense at first. Just try to make a leap from a sound to a word. Maybe your poem will be a list of words or phrases. Don't force it to make rational sense. For example:

> *Wishes on the windowsill.*
> *Touch. Tiger. Touch.*
> *Fling the song through shoots and vines.*

Lingering:

Now imagine you are a scientist explaining what this odd combination of words means. Is this nature's gossip, philosophy, poetry? What kind of people understand this language? What kind of people will never understand it? Should humans learn to speak it? Why or why not?

Art is a lie that makes us realize truth.

~Pablo Picasso

Quick:

Write a poem in the first person in which everything is completely invented. It can be something ordinary or completely fanciful. For example, *I drove to Cincinnati to collect my unemployment check,* or *When my feet first hit the moon's surface, the dust rising nearly blinded me.*

Lingering:

Reel out this invented life as far as you desire. Enjoy using a persona (the Greek word for "mask") to explore situations that you'd be unlikely to encounter in your ordinary life.

April is the cruellest month, breeding
Lilacs out of the dead land, mixing
Memory and desire, stirring
Dull roots with spring rain.
~T.S. Eliot

Quick:

Is April really the cruelest month as T.S. Eliot claims at the beginning of "The Waste Land"? Write two or three lines agreeing or disagreeing with Eliot's famous declaration.

Lingering:

Maybe you want to propose other months that are crueler than April and explain why? Or perhaps you want to question Eliot's gloomy view of spring? Maybe it is not the months of the year that are cruel at all but something else you want to take the time to contemplate.

We hold these truths to be self-evident, that all men are created equal, that they are endowed by their Creator with certain unalienable Rights, that among these are Life, Liberty and the pursuit of Happiness.

~The Declaration of Independence

Quick:

List two poetic truths you hold to be self-evident. For example: *I hold these truths to be self-evident: the air around a crying baby is red; there is a secret, yet-to-be- identified organ, wedged between the stomach and the heart, that releases a hormone into the brain, igniting awe and wonder.*

Lingering:

Continue exploring your poetic truths, letting your imagination reign. If you feel the need for a little grounding, slip a few facts into your poem. Should you be inclined, ponder the nature of truth or perhaps contradictory truths.

Tell me, is the rose naked
or is that her only dress?
                    ~Pablo Neruda

Quick:

In *The Book of Questions*, Chilean poet Pablo Neruda composes poems entirely made up of questions. Take a minute to write your own poem built of questions. You might start with a simple one—*Where did I put my shoes?*—or, if you feel inclined, reach toward more mysterious, bewildering questions like those Neruda asks: *"If I have died and don't know it / Of whom do I ask the time?"*

Lingering:

As you cultivate your questions allow some of them to be perplexing or cryptic. Allow incongruities to merge into surprising juxtapositions.

the poems I have not written
would break the hearts of every
woman who's ever left me
                    ~John Brehm

Quick:

In "The Poems I Have Not Written," John Brehm writes about all the wonderful poems he has yet to produce. Take a minute to contemplate the power of your own unwritten poems. Jot down their magical powers. Be explicit about the ways they would change the world if they were written.

Lingering:

Perhaps you can include a few of the names of the poems you've never written or the circumstances that inspired them. You can remember how they were received at the Kennedy Center, how Oprah's face looked as she read one on national television. Pamper your vanity here and have a great time doing it.

It is an illusion that photos are made with the camera.... they are made with the eye, heart and head.

~Henri Cartier-Bresson

Quick:

Compose a snapshot in words of something that happened in your past, or of something you wish had happened. Imagine you are describing a photograph of the event. Be specific. Describe the place, the people, the quality of the light.

Lingering:

Now describe someone finding this snapshot years later. What would this person say about the event? Would it flood this speaker with memories? Or with a desire to have been a part of what was happening? Or with some other emotion: shame? envy? joy? laughter?

Two Butterflies went out at Noon—
And waltzed above a Farm—
Then stepped straight through the Firmament
And rested on a Beam—
                    ~Emily Dickinson

Quick:

Write about a particular time of day: 6:02 a.m., 3:47 p.m., noon, dawn, or midnight. Try to capture the essence of that time of day with an image, a smell, or perhaps the experience of a human or animal body at that hour.

Lingering:

Now try to capture the opposite of this time of day. Is it exactly twelve hours later? Or is it five minutes later? What is the image, smell, or feeling now?

I learned how to start a poem in a very familiar place and move away from that and use it as a launching pad to abstract territories.

~Billy Collins

Quick:

Start your poem in an ordinary location: your kitchen, your garden, your work desk. Then launch the poem into a fantastical place: Queen Elizabeth's court, outer space, Iceland.

Lingering:

Immerse yourself in your fantastical world—its smells, its sounds, its sights. Make it as real as everything in your ordinary life. Do you fit in? Or are you an outsider? What is the most delicious aspect of this place?

Ink runs from the corners of my mouth.
There is no happiness like mine.

~Mark Strand

Quick:

Imagine eating a poem. What is its texture? Smell? How does it go down? You can be talking about poetry in general, or you may have a very specific poem in mind. If you are thinking of a specific poem, explain how individual words or phrases taste. Are they easily digestible or do they get caught in the throat?

Lingering:

What happens if one eats too much or too little poetry? What is the proper dish or spoon to use to serve it? Why do children love it or hate it? Can it be disguised to make it more palatable?

Poetry is philosophy's sister, the one that wears makeup.
~Jennifer Grotz

Quick:

Write from the point-of-view of a person other than yourself. This may be a fictional character you invent, a person you know, a living person, or even an historical figure. Start with the words, "You'll never believe it, but…"

Lingering:

Develop this persona. Let this character talk about dreams, obsessions, philosophy, and so on. Enjoy moving around in another person's skin.

A poem is like a ghost seeking substantiality, a soul in search of body more appealing than the bare bones mere verses rattle.
~William H. Gass

Quick:

Bring something back to life in a poem. This could be a dead flower, a loved one, a long-lost friend, a distant ancestor, and so on. Let us see it, hear it, understand why you want it back.

Lingering:

Contemplate this life-giving power. Is this bringing-back-to-life consoling? Dangerous? Surprising?

Poetry: three mismatched shoes at the entrance of a dark alley.
~Charles Simic

Quick:

Jot down six favorite words. These can be words that evoke important memories or places (*Tuolumne*, *dunes*) or words whose sounds make you swoon (*scintilla*, *whirly*). Now start writing, weaving your words into the poem as you go. Don't plan how you will use your words, just let your creative unconscious come up with ideas as you write.

Lingering:

Jot down five ugly words, such as *coarse*, *rancid*, *dagger*. Let at least one of these words enter your poem. If you like, add more favorite and more ugly words as you go along and see where each takes you.

The poetry of the earth is never dead.

~John Keats

Quick:

Spend a little time exploring weird facts about the earth:
how much space dust falls to earth each year? how much
of the planet's surface is desert? how much water do we
have on earth? (You can find lots of information by
going to the Web and looking up "amazing facts about
the earth.") Use the facts in a poem.

Lingering:

Write a mirror poem by creating wholly invented "facts"
about the earth. For example, "*the number of redheads in a
landmass equals the number of sunny days per year.*" Let your
ideas roam as freely as you like.

Poetry's a zoo in which you keep demons and angels.
                                                        ~Les Murray

Quick:

Let us hear a conversation in which your angels and your demons state their claims on you. Allow your demons to be appealing, if naughty. And if your angels want to get a little spicy, let them.

Lingering:

Spin out this dialogue into a couple of pages—allow contradictions, confusion, and mystery.

Poetry is the language in which man explores his own amazement.
~Christopher Fry

Quick:

Express your amazement with the world around you. Attend not just to the large, important triumphs (Magna Carta or elephants) but also to the small ones (the little half-moons on your fingernails, a marble, or a hair left in the sink.)

Lingering:

Take time to linger on one of your descriptions, showing this amazing thing in fresh detail. Alternatively, don't describe anything too closely; just create a list that is long and wild and varied.

Star light, star bright,
First star I see tonight,
I wish I may, I wish I might,
Have this wish I wish tonight.

~Anonymous

Quick:

Begin every line of this poem with the phrase "I wish."
Allow material things to come into your poems, but also
spiritual or political or cosmic things as well.

Lingering:

Experiment with bringing some tension into your
wishes: what shouldn't you wish for? does someone
close to you disapprove of your wishes? what happens
when you ask, "What good are wishes?"

A poet's work is to name the unnameable, to point at frauds, to take sides, start arguments, shape the world, and stop it going to sleep.
    ~Salman Rushdie

Quick:

Write a poem of outrage. Take a side, start an argument, expose a fraud. You can admonish someone's bad behavior or stake a claim for a new world order.

Lingering:

Continue to unleash your inner rebel. Defy manners. Yell. Shout. Use giant fonts. Sling your outrage across the entire page.

Oh! kangaroos, sequins, chocolate sodas!
You really are beautiful!
                                      ~Frank O'Hara

Quick:

Frank O'Hara wrote *Lunch Poems* while sitting in Times Square during his lunch hour, absorbing the world around him. Find a time this week (if lunch works, go with that) where you can sit and watch the world around you. Celebrate everything in front of you, from noisy teenagers to trash. Nothing is too insignificant.

Lingering:

Make your celebration even more inclusive by praising as many "unpoetic" things as possible. Think laundromats, trash cans, drainpipes.

Writers don't write from experience, although many are hesitant to admit that they don't. . . if you wrote from experience, you'd get maybe one book, maybe three poems. Writers write from empathy.
~Nikki Giovanni

Quick:

Write a poem from the point-of-view of your enemy. This may be a person, an illness, a government, a temptation.

Lingering:

As you discover your enemy's voice, allow yourself to be surprised. Engage in big philosophical questions if you like: what is the value of an enemy? is hate an extension of love? what have you gained from this enemy? Alternatively, find a way (through magic, if necessary) to transform your enemy into a friend.

A poem is a little machine for remembering itself.
~Don Paterson

Quick:

Write a poem of gratitude to language. Include the words and phrases you love. Celebrate the words that have given themselves to you in poems. What do you want them to know?

Lingering:

Try to describe the physical experience of writing a poem: think not just of your brain but of your muscles, your vertebrae, your lungs, your sinuses, your kneecaps. Show how language inhabits our minds, our bodies, and, if you like, our souls.

The poet doesn't invent. He listens.

~Jean Cocteau

Quick:

Listen to the world around you. Try to capture the rhythms you perceive. Jot down fragments of overheard sounds or conversation that you hear as you wait in line at the bank, sit in a coffee shop, eat lunch at school, and so on. You could include snippets of language from the radio or TV if that seems interesting. You may use something you've heard to start the poem or end it. As you write, let the sounds or fragments enter freely; don't try to muscle them into any particular meaning. Allow them just to appear. Don't feel you must explain them.

Lingering:

Repeat your favorite fragments or sounds throughout the poem. Sometimes restate them in your own words. Think of the repetition as a kind of refrain or echo.

I think that we're beginning to remember that the first poets didn't come out of a classroom, that poetry began when somebody walked off of a savanna or out of a cave and looked up at the sky with wonder and said, "Ahhh." That was the first poem.

~Lucille Clifton

Quick:

Begin by looking at something in the natural world—the sky, as suggested by Lucille Clifton, or the moon, grass, dirt, snow, mountains, an ant, a leaf, a rock. Describe it as if you were the first person ever to see it.

Lingering:

Now allow the thing—the sky, the snow, the ant—to say something directly to you.

Earth laughs in flowers.
                    ~Ralph Waldo Emerson

Quick:

Find a list of poisonous flowers and write down the names that interest or surprise you. Sinister names—*angel's trumpet, bloodflower, false indigo*—might be fun. Sweet-sounding flowers—*buttercup, iris, laceflower*—could take you in another direction. Let your mind explore the idea of the deceptively beautiful.

Lingering:

Look for your favorite flower on the list and contemplate your affection for it. If you discover it is poisonous, do you still love it? If it is not poisonous, do you breathe a sigh of relief or secretly long for just a little danger?

The question is not what you look at, but what you see.
                                    ~Henry David Thoreau

Quick:

Describe an emotion using only images. Let the images float into the poem without explanation.

Lingering:

Find the image you like best and invent a backstory. How did the things or persons in the image get there? Perhaps there is a secret involved or a forgotten story to tell.

A poet is, before anything else, a person who is passionately in love with language.
        ~W.H. Auden

Quick:

List ten words you love. They can be simple words like *brick* or *tie*, or more exotic words like *extraordinarily*, *verminous*, or *lollygagging*. Now start a poem and try to use as many of your words as you can. Don't think about it in advance. Just jump in and see what happens.

Lingering:

Continue the poem by trying to use all of your words a second time, but, if you can, use them in an entirely different way.

Like a piece of ice on a hot stove the poem must ride on its own melting.
  ~Robert Frost

Quick:

Write a poem about a meal, any meal. This may be your favorite meal, an unusual meal, the meal you would make if you went to cooking school, or the worst meal of your life. Use smell and taste and touch as well as sight and sound to capture this culinary event.

Lingering:

Now, take this poem to, as Frost says, "its own melting." I'm not sure what Frost meant by that, so just have fun with it. You know, take it with a grain of salt—which, as it turns out, is both a seasoning for food and another way to melt ice.

Poetry is finer and more philosophical than history; for poetry expresses the universal, and history only the particular.

~Aristotle

Quick:

Go to onthisday.com and look up the historical events that took place on a date that is important to you. Pick one you think might have poetic possibilities. I quite liked one for April 7, 1827—English chemist John Walker invents wooden matches! The event doesn't have to be the subject, but let the event come into the poem in some way.

Lingering:

Pick another event from the same day and compose another poem. If it sounds fun, try interweaving the two poems.

Only those who will risk going too far can possibly find out how far one can go.
~T.S. Eliot

Quick:

Risk going too far today by writing in very long lines. Oh, and start each line with the phrase "I remember." Try to include as many specific images as possible. Allow yourself to linger on tiny details—not just the cat, but his *striped tail, the pink triangle of his nose, eight gray whiskers, nails as transparent as onions, a cry that floats into the leaves of the newly budding lilac….*

Lingering:

Continue the poem, but this time begin each long line with *I have probably forgotten*. Try writing a section that alternates between what you remember and what you seem to have forgotten.

A poem begins as a lump in the throat, a sense of wrong, a homesickness, a lovesickness.
~Robert Frost

Quick:

Write about something that gives you a lump in the throat. Is it caused by being wronged? By missing someone? Explore the idea of longing as fully as you can.

Lingering:

Give your longing a shape. Is your longing like a cage? A case of influenza? A cold moon? Black ice? A tornado? See how fully you can develop your metaphor.

Poetry is eternal graffiti written in the heart of everyone.
~Lawrence Ferlinghetti

Quick:

Write very short love poems—each one should be just five or six words long. Imagine them as graffiti spray-painted over your page. Explode them across the white space with bright images and vibrant language just as graffiti dazzles a wall.

Lingering:

Use one of these short poems to begin a longer poem about love. Weave the other short poems into the long one.

Genuine poetry can communicate before it is understood.
                                                    ~T.S. Eliot

Quick:

Write with absolute freedom anything that pops into your mind. The only rule here is to try to be as nonsensical as possible. Incline toward gibberish. The sillier the better.

Lingering:

Highlight all the phrases you love from your gibberish and reorganize them into a new poem. Add connecting words if you like, but don't feel obligated. Repeat phrases or words that really appeal to you. Come back to this poem in a week and see if it communicates something to you that you may not have understood when you were writing it.

We mustn't prejudge the past.
~William Whitelaw

Quick:

Tell a story from your past. It can be a dramatic story or simply a poignant one. A childhood adventure. Meeting your true love. Being stood up at the prom.

Lingering:

Now tell the same story from someone else's point of view. Let them explain what happened as they understood it. What they hope you learned from it. What they would have done in your shoes.

Poetry lies its way to the truth.
~John Ciardi

Quick:

Write a poem that takes place in your actual house but that is completely invented. You might start at the breakfast table eating Cheerios, but somewhere a French-speaking tiger enters and starts reciting nursery rhymes.

Lingering:

Let more crazy things enter your house, creating happiness or havoc. As you let your fancy run wild, always ground the action in the actual geography of your home.

For what is a poem but a hazardous attempt at self-understanding? It is the deepest part of autobiography?
~Robert Penn Warren

Quick:

Write ten lines beginning with the words "I love…."

Lingering:

Now describe your earliest memories. Don't try to explain them or make sense of them, just describe them as if they were a series of snapshots. Weave together your memories and your ten lines in a way that pleases you.

Spring has returned. The earth resembles a little girl who has memorized many poems.
~Rainer Maria Rilke

Quick:

Write a poem that explains how spring was invented. Who created it? A person, an animal, a god? Was it created on purpose or accidentally? You might include details about the creation process: did it include fire, air, water, or gnats? Consider telling why it was necessary to invent spring.

Lingering:

Did spring turn out as planned or did the creation go awry in some way? Ponder a few problems with spring such as flooding, pollen, late snowstorms, or anything that you find troublesome. Should spring be continued or abolished?

Poetry is an act of peace.
                    ~Pablo Neruda

Quick:

Write a poem that forgives. You might forgive a person for doing something hurtful, or you might forgive a storm for creating too much snow, or you might forgive your legs for being too short, or you might forgive your dog for not being able to speak English.

Lingering:

Imagine the ways forgiving changes the forgiver. Does it alter consciousness? Does it rearrange the human cellular structure? Let your ruminations be wild.

The poet is the priest of the invisible.
~Wallace Stevens

Quick:

Look up the origin of your family name. If your name is not listed, try your mother's or your grandmother's maiden name. Now imagine the world that invented your family name. What does it look like? What kind of people inhabit it? How did your name come about? No need to be historically or geographically accurate.

Lingering:

Now look up a name you wish you had. Imagine who you would be with this name. Be quite specific about how it would change your appearance, life, loves, and pastimes.

I do not ask the wounded person how he feels, I myself become the wounded person.
~Walt Whitman

Quick:

Write about a tragic experience you only know second-hand. It may be a story a friend has told you, or it may be something you have read. One rule: write in the first person, as though this experience was your own.

Lingering:

Allow yourself to dig deep. Draw on all your senses. Give yourself permission to add details that may or may not be factually true. Explain something about the event that no one else knows.

All poets, all writers are political. They either maintain the status quo, or they say, "Something's wrong, let's change it for the better."
    ~Sonia Sanchez

Quick:

Write a poem in which you take a stand about something that is important to you. Allow yourself to use strong language, write only in capital letters, change the font size, or do whatever else gets the intensity of your feelings on the page.

Lingering:

Now try to write about the same issue as quietly as possible—hedge your bets, change your mind, question your intentions, and so on.

Writing poetry is a state of free float.
                                    ~Margaret Atwood

Quick:

Let your words float across the page like a boat unmoored from its dock. Let your mind free associate until you find a current you like, then let that current take you where it will. Use lots of space between words. Let the poem use up the entire page.

Lingering:

Return to your free association. Once again, drift until another current finds you. Repeat the process as many times as you like.

A single day is enough to make us a little larger or, another time, a little smaller.
    ~Paul Klee

Quick:

Write a poem about something very small. This could be a tiny stone, a seed, a little animal, a piece of dust, a single word—whatever you like.

Lingering:

Imagine how this small thing could create dramatic consequences. These might be true or pure fabrication.

Don't use the telephone.
People are never ready to answer it.
Use poetry.
            ~Jack Kerouac

Quick:

Write a poem to someone instead of calling. Let your language be friendly, if that's how you feel. Or let it be serious if you are calling about a serious matter. Be gossipy if there's something juicy you must share.

Lingering:

Say something in your poem that you wouldn't dare say on the phone.

Poetry heals the wounds inflicted by reason.
                                                    ~Novalis

Quick:

Write a poem about yourself in which nothing is true.

Lingering:

List five words about yourself that capture your essence:
for example, *friendly*, *curious*, *shy*. Now use each of those
words in a poem. Caveat: do not use your five words to
describe yourself but something in the world around
you—a curious ant, a shy rose, a friendly question from
a neighbor.

I don't create poetry, I create myself, for me my poems are a way to me.
    ~Edith Södergran

Quick:

Ponder your future by beginning several lines with *I wonder if I will ever...*

Lingering:

Now write responses for each line. Start each one with *If not, I'll...* Let your responses alternate between being realistic and being wonderfully improbable.

I grew up in this town, my poetry was born between the hill and the river, it took its voice from the rain, and like the timber, it steeped itself in the forests.

~Pablo Neruda

Quick:

Think of a place you know very well. Perhaps it is a place you have lived recently or perhaps a place from your childhood. If it is a rural place, make a list of all the mountains, rivers, valleys, or other natural features you can think of. If it is an urban place, list the streets, the shops, the schools, and so on. Try to come up with at least ten specific names related to your place. Now use them all in a poem about home.

Lingering:

Now weave your memories about this place into the poem. The memories can be chatty and friendly, or they can be fragmented and dreamlike—or everything all at once!

Poets have been mysteriously silent on the subject of cheese.
~G.K. Chesterton

Quick:

Write a poem in honor of cheese. You can choose any kind of cheese—fancy French cheeses or Kraft singles. Whatever cheese you choose, be convincing about its virtues, either genuine or invented.

Lingering:

Meditate on the condition of a world without cheese. Hyperbole—exaggerated claims that are not meant to be taken literally—may be called for here.

Poetry is what in a poem makes you laugh, cry, prickle, be silent, makes your toe nails twinkle, makes you want to do this or that or nothing, makes you know that you are alone and not alone in the unknown world, that your bliss and suffering is forever shared and forever all your own.

~Dylan Thomas

Quick:

Describe how your favorite poems make you feel. Do they make your toenails twinkle, as Thomas suggests? Be attentive to their visceral effects on your body. Do your poems create tingling, weight, lightness, darkness, heaving, quacking, or jitters in your shoulders, hips, gut, eyebrows? Do they incite you to dance the tango, walk barefoot in new grass, drink a gin and tonic?

Lingering:

Explore the ways these poems have affected you by engaging a metaphor. Start each line with "I am" then find an object that registers your experience. For example, *I am a stone, I am a new leaf, I am the throat of the song bird, I am clouds heavy with rain.* If you like, cut up what you've written into individual lines and weave them together in a new order.

My mistress' eyes are nothing like the sun;
Coral is far more red than her lips' red;
If snow be white, why then her breasts are dun;
If hairs be wires, black wires grow on her head.
I have seen roses damasked, red and white,
But no such roses see I in her cheeks;

~William Shakespeare

Quick:

Think of someone or something you love and catalogue his/her/their/its imperfections. They can be physical, behavioral, psychological, and so on. They can be serious or utterly frivolous. Maybe you want to use the person's/creature's/thing's name in the poem. If you want, you could even address the poem to the person/creature/thing. For example: *Rob, your eyebrows are uneven, your shirt is always wrinkled…*

Lingering:

Now say why you love this person/creature/thing anyway. Be very specific. Show the object of your affection in all his/her/their/its flawed glory: *Fido, I can't stop loving the spray of black spots across your snout…*

maybe a splash of water on the face,
a palmful of vitamins—
but mostly buzzing around the house on espresso
                                        ~Billy Collins

Quick:

Describe a perfectly ordinary morning in your world, aiming to capture every ordinary detail. What sounds do you hear? What sights do you see? Are there familiar smells in the air? What is your normal morning routine? Is the radio on? Does your heater make noise? Your dishwasher? Is laundry sloshing around? Do creatures call for your attention? Do you wear slippers? Yes, think of all the mundane details and write them down. Use plain and simple language.

Lingering:

Anticipate what will be going on at noon, at six, at bedtime. If you like, imagine something totally unexpected shaking up your routine. What would it be? How would you react?

Poetry is the journal of a sea animal living on land, wanting to fly in the air.
        ~Carl Sandburg

Quick:

Begin by describing a place that feels like your "real" home—even if you've never been there. This can be an actual place you know or an imaginary place. Your "place" may even be in a different time period. Evoke its essence through sight, smell, or hearing. Capture the heart of your yearning for this place.

Lingering:

Try imagining how your life would change if you lived in this place. What new powers would you have? What dreams would be fulfilled? Would there be a dark side you hadn't anticipated?

O my Luve's like a red, red rose,
  That's newly sprung in June:
O my Luve's like the melodie,
  That's sweetly play'd in tune.

~Robert Burns

Quick:

What is your love like? A GPS system? A jazz tune? An overcoat? Why is it like this thing? Does it help you find your way? Syncopate your heart? Keep you warm? Feel free to explore one comparison in depth (*my heart is like a jazz tune / it syncopates / plays havoc with my pulse / till I'm Buddy Rich's drum, thump-a-thump-a-thump thump thump*) or to do as Burns does and make lots of different comparisons.

Lingering:

Explain why your love is better than any other love. Try using comparisons: *if your love were a drug it would cure cancer, if it were a ladder it would reach Cassiopeia, if it were a song it would stay at number one on the charts until people couldn't remember any other songs.*

Poets are soldiers that liberate words from the steadfast possession of definition.
  ~Eli Khamarov

Quick:

Transform a few words from their usual definitions by making verbs out of nouns. We already have some great words that do that: *swanning, partying, dogging.* Create some new verbs, even if they sound odd at first. (Animals and bugs are quite useful here: what would *caterpillering around* mean? *Deering? Spiderizing? Gnatting?*) Write several very short poems (just three or four lines each) and use one of your new verbs in each one.

Lingering:

If you dare, throw in a couple of words that are complete inventions (*gazenter, rotable, textsplaining* come to mind). Can you use your new word in such a way that the reader understands what it might mean from the context?

Poetry is not an expression of the party line. It's that time of night, lying in bed, thinking what you really think, making the private world public, that's what the poet does.

~Allen Ginsberg

Quick:

Take for your topic something you consider very private. This may be quite small or silly (for example, your secret passion for Big Macs), something substantial (a strongly held but unpopular conviction), or perhaps even a family secret. Use your poem to explore this private information. Write as if you are talking to yourself in the middle of night. Give all the important information, even as you seem reluctant to confess it.

Lingering:

Explain how revealing this private information changes the world. Does it make people mad? Does it mean you'll have to pay a fine? Or does it alter the orbit of planets or the color of the sky? Don't be afraid to be bold.

Come live with me and be my Love,
And we will all the pleasures prove,
That hills and valleys, dale and field,
And all the craggy mountains yield…

There will I make thee beds of roses
And a thousand fragrant posies,
A cap of flowers, and a kirtle
Embroider'd all with leaves of myrtle.

A gown made of the finest wool
Which from our pretty lambs we pull,
Fair linèd slippers for the cold,
With buckles of the purest gold.

A belt of straw and ivy buds
With coral clasps and amber studs…

~Christopher Marlowe

Quick:

Create clothes for your beloved in a poem using things in your ordinary world. These should be things that you love, even if they are not conventional items used for clothing. You may choose things from your kitchen (dish towels, spoons, colanders, iceberg lettuce) or perhaps from your car, your office, your gym, your book club, your coffee shop, your tap room, and so on. The idea here is to be fanciful.

Lingering:

Now imagine going out on the town together. Jot down the comments you hear from passersby. What would bankers think? Mail carriers? Teenagers? What does your beloved have to say about this attire?

Poets are the unacknowledged legislators of the world.
~Percy Bysshe Shelley

Quick:

Write a poem in the form of a congressional bill. Give it a number if you like (HR007, S222). Use the word "Act" in the title. Let the bill address something important to you, but something that cannot be legislated, the more outrageous the better. For example, consider a bill allowing house cats to look like zebras or one that eliminates winter.

Lingering:

Add some slogans that might be used in a campaign to promote your bill. Include a stump speech in support of it.

Poetry is an echo, asking a shadow dancer to be a partner.
~Carl Sandburg

Quick:

Pirates have stranded you on a desert island. Describe your thoughts and feelings about being stranded, your plans to survive, and your hopes for rescue.

Lingering:

What book did you grab before you were forced down the gangplank? Writing in the voice of a character from this book, create a response. Does this character give moral support? Practical advice? Does it scold you? Tell you a story to pass the time?

Shall I compare thee to a summer's day?
Thou art more lovely and more temperate.

~William Shakespeare

Quick:

Compare someone you love or someone you hate to a summer's day. This might be a beautiful day or it might be a stormed-tossed, windy, lightning-filled one.

Lingering:

What happens to this person at night? Does he or she have an alternate personality that no one knows but you? Reveal all!

There is poetry as soon as we realize that we possess nothing.
~John Cage

Quick:

Make a short list of things you've lost—lovers, keys, pets, homes, friends, and so on. Now write a poem addressed to one of these, explaining what you think happened. This can be serious or it can be outrageous and silly.

Lingering:

Now consider the consequences of this loss. How did it affect you or perhaps someone else? Again, write seriously or ridiculously. Once you've explained all the gruesome or hilarious details, apologize for the loss or justify it.

A weed is but an unloved flower.
                                    ~Ella Wheeler Wilcox

Quick:

Write about something you don't like—a weed, the nasty dog next door, skim milk—or someone—the sour-faced bank teller, the football coach, the noisy neighbor. Be specific about what you hate: that grimacing smile, the orange necktie.

Lingering:

Now refocus your observations on what might be good about this person or thing: the bills she doles out are always crisp; he bakes your favorite cookies. Is this weed more like a flower? Explain why you can see this person/thing now as a flower or why he/she/they/it will always be a weed.

I love the man that can smile in trouble, that can gather strength from distress, and grow brave by reflection.

~Thomas Paine

Quick:

Using as much humor as possible, tell the story of a day when everything goes wrong: you run out of coffee, the car battery is dead, you miss the bus, and so on. Hint—things can happen to you in your poem that have never happened to you in life.

Lingering:

Pile it on. Be wild and extravagant. Have fun making trouble. Maybe a case of mistaken identity? Losing a winning lottery ticket? Then argue for the unrecognized benefits of bad days.

Poetry is everywhere; it just needs editing.
~James Tate

Quick:

Take one of the poems you have written and edit it down to no more than twenty words. You may edit it any way you like—cut whole lines if you wish, or trim individual words. The goal is to get a tight twenty words.

Lingering:

Use the new twenty-word poem as the starting place for a new poem. Write a page or more. Now edit this new section down to twenty words. If it amuses you, try weaving the two twenty-word poems together.

When god decided to invent
everything he took one
breath bigger than a circustent
and everything began

~E. E. Cummings

Quick:

Reinvent yourself. Ponder small changes—how you might take up gardening, for example—and dramatize your transformation. Describe yourself in the nursery buying seeds, or in the yard tilling the ground, weeding, tending, and harvesting. Or imagine a vast, profound, or whimsical change: you become an astronaut, a different gender, a planet, a giraffe. Involve readers in the transformation as concretely as possible.

Lingering:

Think back a moment to your old life now that you are something new. Do you miss anything? Were there any advantages of your old life? Or is this new life the real deal?

Poetry is language in orbit.
                              ~Seamus Heaney

Quick:

Start with the words "if only" and go from there. Whenever you get stuck, repeat "if only." As you write, try to use as much of the space on the page as possible. Don't increase your font, just spread the words on the page like stars and galaxies in the sky.

Lingering:

Continue your orbit by using "when" or "although" to start new lines.

Through the open doors
The harmless phantoms on their errands glide,
With feet that make no sound upon the floors.

~Henry Wadsworth Longfellow

Quick:

Write about a ghost. This can be any kind of ghost: the ghost of person, the ghost of an idea. How do you know it is there? How does it speak? What does it want from you?

Lingering:

Imagine your ghost as someone who helps—perhaps as your therapist or personal shopper. Have fun inventing ways it helps and/or hinders you. Finally, ponder the benefits of having a ghost, or explain why it should be exorcised.

Why not walk in the aura of magic that gives to the small things in life their uniqueness and importance?

~Germaine Greer

Quick:

Record one of your small joys. For example, cutting a tulip from your garden and putting it in a vase on your desk, tasting a fresh raspberry, taking your first sip of coffee in the morning, watching the sun go down, walking your dog. Don't record any emotion here, just the act itself. Be as precise as possible. Try to include sounds, smells, and sensations as well as images.

Lingering:

Write a few lines celebrating your small joy. Explain why it is better than big happiness. Tease out the uniqueness of your small joy in any way that appeals to you: is it connected to physical pleasure? To a delightful memory? Tell us everything you can about its importance.

To love oneself is the beginning of a lifelong romance.

~Oscar Wilde

Quick:

Shamelessly brag about your extraordinariness. (Remember, no one else needs to see this.) Have fun saying how great you are, how talented, how brilliant, how tall. The point here is joyous abundance.

Lingering:

Turn your imperfections into perfections: celebrate your bad knee, your crooked eyebrow, your wrinkles, your imperfect pitch.

At some point in life the world's beauty becomes enough. You don't need to photograph, paint, or even remember it. It is enough.
~Toni Morrison

Quick:

Focus on one beautiful thing in the world and describe it as carefully as you can. This can be a sight, a sound, a smell, a thought, a relationship, a memory. In other words, anything at all that is beautiful to you.

Lingering:

See if you can figure out why, as Morrison says, "it is enough." Or, explain why, despite its beauty, it isn't enough.

Heaven is under our feet as well as over our heads.
                                        ~Henry David Thoreau

Quick:

Describe the heavenly and not so heavenly elements of the natural world in your neighborhood. Note lots of things you love (the maples turning in the fall, for example) but also include natural things you don't like so much (wasps, your neighbor's dog poop on your grass).

Lingering:

End the poem with three lines that all begin, "If heaven includes both [something you like] and [something you don't like], then…." For example, *If heaven includes both chickadees and stinging nettle, then I will bloom and carry calamine lotion.* Use unexpected, suggestive verbs: *calibrate, lunge, qualify, bombast…*

Nothing is more revealing than movement.

~Martha Graham

Quick:

Dance words across the page. The catch? Don't try to control the words or force them to make sense. Use lots of space. Pretend you are the Jackson Pollock of poetry spilling words every which way.

Lingering:

Select some of the words you've danced across the page and use them in a more ordinary line. But don't let the line be too ordinary—let it start in the middle of the page or way over on the right side. Use space in your poem in ways you've never tried before.

Are we to paint what is on the face, what's inside the face, or what's behind it?
                    ~Picasso

Quick:

Describe someone's face. This can be a friend, a family member, an acquaintance, a stranger, a celebrity, an historical figure—anyone at all, but it must be a real person. Now try to capture what's behind the face. Your thoughts might be based in reality—some piece of information you have about the person—or you may be completely speculative. Let yourself be daring in what you imagine.

Lingering:

List several names and create exterior/interior portraits for each. Did the face shape the personality? Or did the personality shape the face?

A child said, What is the grass? fetching it to me with full
     hands;
How could I answer the child.... I do not know what it is
     any more than he.
                    ~Walt Whitman

Quick:

Ponder a childlike question: why is the sky blue? why are
there no more dinosaurs? why do we sleep? The best
questions may be the ones about which you know very
little. Invent an answer that has nothing to do with fact.

Lingering:

Look up possible answers to your question. Use as much
or as little factual information as you like to continue the
poem. Consider stretching the factual until it becomes
fantastical.

It's just cheatgrass, my dear,
with a funny trick.
                    ~Cara Chamberlain

Quick:

Write a poem explaining what something is or how to do something. Caveat: address your reader directly, as Cara Chamberlain does above.

Lingering:

Address your reader with increasing intimacy as you develop your poem. Let your word choice reveal your attitude toward your reader: are you condescending, courteous, jokey, rude, sycophantic?

Walt Whitman, a kosmos, of Manhattan the son,
Turbulent, fleshy, sensual, eating, drinking and breeding,
No sentimentalist, no stander above men and women or
apart from them,
No more modest than immodest.

~Walt Whitman

Quick:

Write your name. Now define yourself. Say where you're from. List adjectives that describe you. List the things you do or don't do. Compose a portrait of your character by saying not just what you are but also what you are not.

Lingering:

Explain to your readers how they can find you. Where will you be? What will you be doing? Who will be with you? What should they do if they can't find you?

Surprising how glass shoes carry you
past orchestra and sparkling gowns
down marble stairs. You lift your skirt
for speed, the fabric a sail in your wake.
The clock strikes. Your heart hesitates.

~Tami Haaland

Quick:

Think of a fairytale and put yourself in the place of the main character. You are Cinderella, Rapunzel, Jack (or even his beanstalk). Now write a poem from that perspective but use the second person to tell the story, as Tami Haaland does above. For example, *You pull the bean from your pocket. You stick your finger in the dirt.*

Lingering:

End the poem by questioning parts of the experience. Not "Did this really happen?" but *Was it the dirt that called my name, or the bean seed?*

His mom buys him a truck
for his sweet sixteen b-day.
And a tattoo
on his right ankle.

~Lowell Jaeger

Quick:

Write a poem about a relative. Let us really see this person. Show him or her or them in action. Odd or eccentric relatives yield very interesting insights.

Lingering:

End the poem by considering the ways you are not like your relative. Or you might mention similarities you'd prefer to forget. You could say why you secretly admire this person, even though others might think him or her or them a terrible role model.

Hey, I wasn't one of those kids
  that put peanut butter
    in your shoes
Just to make you think, or squeezed
    the frog's head into your glass of milk.

~Dave Caserio

Quick:

What kind of kid were you? What kind of things did you like to do—or refuse to do? What did you like to wear or eat? What did you think of bedtime, your parents, animals, TV, your brothers and sisters, and so on?

Lingering:

Now say what kind of kid you weren't. Or, if you want, start with the kind of kid you weren't, then say the kind of kid you were. Or alternate a few lines describing who you were with a few saying who you were not.

Most people ignore most poetry because most poetry ignores most people.
    ~Adrian Mitchell

Quick:

Address a specific person—your mother, a friend, or an acquaintance—in this poem. To get yourself started, use the line, "I've been wanting to tell you," and go from there. Don't worry in advance what you will say. Just write as if you were talking face-to-face.

Lingering:

Now address other people you know. Talk to just a few or a lot of them. Consider aiming some comments at large groups of people: anglers, bowlers, Baptists, poets, teenagers, and so on. Ask them questions. Tell them you don't like the way they wear their hats. Tell them their horoscopes for this week. The goal here is to turn your poetic attention to "most people" in any way that amuses you.

Poems and Quotations

Anonymous: "Star light star bright"

Aristotle: *Poetics*

Margaret Atwood: *Waltzing Again: New and Selected
  Conversations with Margaret Atwood*

W.H. Auden: *New York Times,* 9 October, 1960

Marianne Boruch: "Heavy Lifting"

John Brehm: "The Poems I Have Not Written"

Robert Burns: "A Red Red Rose"

John Cage: *For the Birds*

Henri Cartier-Bresson: *The Decisive Moment*

Dave Caserio: "Maybe It's Mustard or Maybe It's Jam"

Cara Chamberlain: "The Wrathful: Cheatgrass"

G.K. Chesterton: "Cheese"

John Ciardi: "The Writing of Nonfiction Prose"

Lucille Clifton: *Bill Moyers Journal,* 26 February 2010

Jean Cocteau: *Writers at Work: The Paris Review Interviews*

Billy Collins: "Region's Poets Convey a Sense of Place," *New
  York Times,* 1 January 2009; "Morning"

E.E. Cummings: "when god decided to invent"

Emily Dickinson: "Two Butterflies went out at Noon"

John Donne: "The Sun Rising"

T.S. Eliot: "The Waste Land"; Preface to Harry Crosby's
  Transit of Venus; "Dante"

Ralph Waldo Emerson: "Hamatreya"

Lawrence Ferlinghetti: "Americus"

Robert Frost: "The Figure a Poem Makes"; letter to Louis
  Untermeyer, 1 January 1916

Christopher Fry: *Time,* 3 April 1950.

William Gass: "Rilke's Rodin"

Allen Ginsberg: *Ginsberg: A Biography*

Nikki Giovanni: "Conversations with Nikki Giovanni" by Claudia
  Tate

Martha Graham: "The American Dance"

Germaine Greer: *The Change*

Jennifer Grotz: *Here Comes Everybody* blog, April 2005

Tami Haaland: "To Cinderella on the Stair"

Hafiz the Great Sufi Master: "What Do White Birds Say"

Seamus Heaney: *Sunday Independent*, 25 September 1994

Lowell Jaeger: "Real Life"

John Keats: "On the Grasshopper and Cricket"

Jack Kerouac: "To Edward Dahlberg"

Eli Khamarov: *The Shadow Zone*

Paul Klee: *The Diaries of Paul Klee, 1898-1918*

Bruce Lanksy: "I Can't Write a Poem"

Henry Wadsworth Longfellow: "Haunted Houses"

Christopher Marlowe: "The Passionate Shepherd to His Love"

John Milton: *Paradise Lost*

Adrian Mitchell: Preface to *Poems*

Toni Morrison: *Tar Baby*

Les Murray: *The Australian,* 10 May 1997

Pablo Neruda: "Book of Questions, III"; *Memoirs*

Novalis (*aka* Georg Philipp Friedrich Freiherr von Hardenberg):
      "Detached Thoughts"

Frank O'Hara: "Today"

Thomas Paine: *The American Crisis*

Don Paterson: "Memory"

Pablo Picasso: "Picasso Speaks"; *Picasso on Art*

Liam Rector: "An Interview by Sarah Canning"

Rainer Maria Rilke: "Sonnets to Orpheus, First Part: XXI"

Salman Rushdie: *The Satanic Verses*

Sonia Sanchez: "'As Poets, As Activists': An Interview with Sonia
      Sanchez" by David Reich

Carl Sandberg: "Tentative (First Model) Definitions of Poetry";
      "Poetry Reconsidered"

William Shakespeare: "My mistress' eyes are nothing like the
      sun" (Sonnet 130); "Shall I compare thee to a summer's
      day?" (Sonnet 18)

Percy Bysshe Shelley: "Defence of Poetry"

Charles Simic: "Our Angelic Ancestor"

Edith Södergran: "Vierge Moderne"

William Stafford: "A Way of Writing"

Wallace Stevens: "Adagia"

Mark Strand: "Eating Poetry"

James Tate: *The Route as Briefed*

Dylan Thomas: 1951 Letter to a Student

Henry David Thoreau: Journal, 5 August 1851; "The Pond in
Winter," *Walden*

Robert Penn Warren: *New York Times*, 12 May 1985

Ella Wheeler: Wilcox: "I Love You"; "The Weed"

William Whitelaw: *The Times*, 2 July 1999

Walt Whitman: "Song of Myself" 33, 6, 24

Oscar Wilde: *An Ideal Husband*

Danell Jones has taught literature and creative writing for more than thirty years. Her poetry, fiction, essays, and reviews have appeared in various publications including the *Denver Quarterly*, *Beyond Baroque*, *Red River Review*, *Gingko Tree Review*, *Sow's Ear Poetry Review*, *Tonopah Review*, and *Literature and History*. Jones earned a Ph.D. in Literature from Columbia University, where she was awarded a Whiting Fellowship in the Humanities and a Bennett Cerf Award for her work on Virginia Woolf. She was the winner of the Jovanovich prize for poetry from the University of Colorado and has been a finalist for both the Breadloaf Writers' Conference Poetry Prize and the PEN/Nelson Algren in Fiction. Her chapbook of poetry inspired by life in the Mojave entitled *Desert Elegies* was a finalist for New Women's Voices Series. She is the author of two books: *The Virginia Woolf Writers' Workshop: Seven Lessons to Inspire Great Writing* and *An African in Imperial London: The Indomitable Life of A.B.C. Merriman-Labor*, winner of the High Plains Book Award for Nonfiction.

Publications by Two Sylvias Press:

The Daily Poet: Day-By-Day Prompts For Your Writing Practice
by Kelli Russell Agodon and Martha Silano (Print and eBook)

The Daily Poet Companion Journal (Print)

Everything is Writable: 240 Poetry Prompts from Two Sylvias Press
by Kelli Russell Agodon & Annette Spaulding-Convy (Print)

Fire On Her Tongue: An Anthology of Contemporary Women's Poetry edited by Kelli Russell Agodon and Annette Spaulding-Convy (Print and eBook)

The Poet Tarot and Guidebook: A Deck Of Creative Exploration (Print)

The Whimsical Muse: Poetic Play for Busy Creatives by Danell Jones (Print)

Deathbed Sext, Winner of the 2019 Two Sylvias Press Chapbook Prize by Christopher Salerno (Print)

Crown of Wild, Winner of the 2018 Two Sylvias Press Wilder Prize by Erica Bodwell (Print)

American Zero, Winner of the 2018 Two Sylvias Press Chapbook Prize by Stella Wong (Print and eBook)

The Inspired Poet: Writing Exercises to Spark New Work by Susan Landgraf (Print)

All Transparent Things Need Thundershirts, Winner of the 2017 Two Sylvias Press Wilder Prize by Dana Roeser (Print and eBook)

Where The Horse Takes Wing: The Uncollected Poems of Madeline DeFrees edited by Anne McDuffie (Print and eBook)

In The House Of My Father, Winner of the 2017 Two Sylvias Press Chapbook Prize by Hiwot Adilow (Print and eBook)

Box, Winner of the 2017 Two Sylvias Press Poetry Prize by Sue D. Burton (Print and eBook)

Tsigan: The Gypsy Poem (New Edition) by Cecilia Woloch (Print)

PR For Poets by Jeannine Hall Gailey (Print and eBook)

Appalachians Run Amok, Winner of the 2016 Two Sylvias Press Wilder Prize by Adrian Blevins (Print and eBook)

Pass It On! by Gloria J. McEwen Burgess (Print)

Killing Marias by Claudia Castro Luna (Print and eBook)

The Ego and the Empiricist, Finalist 2016 Two Sylvias Press Chapbook Prize by Derek Mong (Print and eBook)

The Authenticity Experiment by Kate Carroll de Gutes (Print and eBook)

Mytheria, Finalist 2015 Two Sylvias Press Wilder Prize by Molly Tenenbaum (Print and eBook)

Arab in Newsland , Winner of the 2016 Two Sylvias Press Chapbook Prize by Lena Khalaf Tuffaha (Print and eBook)

The Blue Black Wet of Wood, Winner of the 2015 Two Sylvias Press Wilder Prize by Carmen R. Gillespie (Print and eBook)

Fire Girl: Essays on India, America, and the In-Between by Sayantani Dasgupta (Print and eBook)

Blood Song by Michael Schmeltzer (Print and eBook)

Naming The No-Name Woman, Winner of the 2015 Two Sylvias Press Chapbook Prize by Jasmine An (Print and eBook)

Community Chest by Natalie Serber (Print)

Phantom Son: A Mother's Story of Surrender by Sharon Estill Taylor (Print and eBook)

What The Truth Tastes Like by Martha Silano (Print and eBook)

landscape/heartbreak by Michelle Peñaloza (Print and eBook)

Earth, Winner of the 2014 Two Sylvias Press Chapbook Prize by Cecilia Woloch (Print and eBook)

The Cardiologist's Daughter by Natasha Kochicheril Moni (Print and eBook)

She Returns to the Floating World by Jeannine Hall Gailey (Print and eBook)

Hourglass Museum by Kelli Russell Agodon (eBook)

Cloud Pharmacy by Susan Rich (eBook)

Dear Alzheimer's: A Caregiver's Diary & Poems by Esther Altshul Helfgott (eBook)

Listening to Mozart: Poems of Alzheimer's by Esther Altshul Helfgott (eBook)

Crab Creek Review 30th Anniversary Issue featuring Northwest Poets edited by Kelli Russell Agodon and Annette Spaulding-Convy (eBook)

Play - this page is my playground
Once you start getting words on the page,
The fun begins

Made in the USA
Coppell, TX
12 November 2020